Rookie Read-About™ Science

Feeling Things

By Allan Fowler

Images supplied by VALAN Photos

Consultants:
Robert L. Hillerich, Ph.D., Bowling Green
State University, Bowling Green, Ohio

Mary Nalbandian, Director of Science,
Chicago Public Schools, Chicago, Illinois

Fay Robinson, Child Development Specialist

CHILDRENS PRESS®
CHICAGO

Series cover and interior design by Sara Shelton

Library of Congress Cataloging-in-Publication Data

Fowler, Allan.
   Feeling things / by Allan Fowler.
     p.   cm.—(Rookie read-about science)
   Summary: Discusses the sense of touch and how it works to tell us more about the world around us.
   ISBN 0-516-04908-9
   1. Touch—Juvenile literature. [1. Touch. 2. Senses and sensation.] I. Title. II. Series.
QP451.F69 1991
152.1'82—dc20   90-22526
                                                    CIP
                                                      AC

Ahh! You stroke a soft
warm kitten and it feels
very good.

Ouch! You stub your toe and it hurts!

What tells you how soft
the kitten feels? What tells
you that your toe hurts
when you stub it?

Your sense of touch
tells you.

You have four other senses. Besides touch,

you see with your eyes.

You hear with your ears.

You smell with your nose.

And you taste with your
tongue.

But your sense of touch is different, because you can feel things with every part of your body, from head to toe.

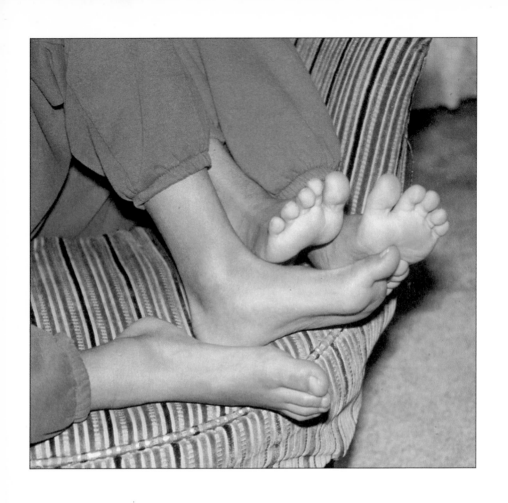

Are the bottoms of your
feet ticklish?

Your sense of touch tells you.

And it tells you that a cool swim on a hot day feels good all over.

Your sense of touch tells you if something is

as hard as a rock

or as soft as a bird's feather

as rough as a tree trunk

or as smooth as glass

as wet as a puddle

or as dry as sand.

You often feel several things at a time when you use your sense of touch.

This ice cube is hard and
cold and wet all at once.

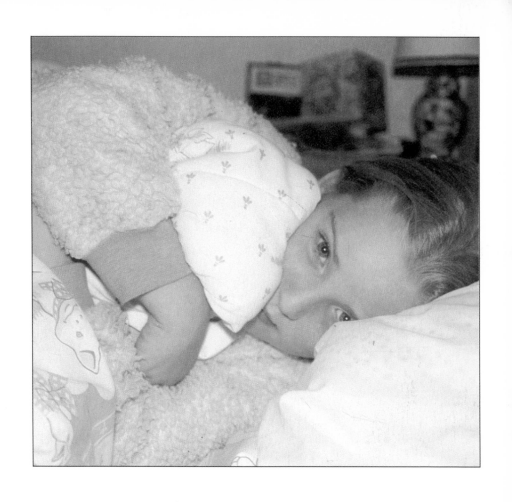

The blanket is soft and
warm and dry.

You must be careful not to touch things that might hurt you like a hot stove or sharp knife.

And don't you think it would feel much better to pet a puppy

than it would to pet a
porcupine?

Words You Know

sense of touch

hard

soft

rough

smooth

wet

dry

hot

cold

Index

About the Author

Allan Fowler is a free-lance writer with a background in advertising. Born in New York, he lives in Chicago now and enjoys traveling.

Photo Credits

PhotoEdit—Myrleen Ferguson, Cover
Valan—© V. Wilkinson, 3, 8, 9, 10, 12, 20, 24, 25, 30 (top left & bottom right), 31 (top right); © Wouterloot-Gregoire, 4, 30 (bottom left); © Kennon Cooke, 7, 17, 31 (bottom left); © Jean Bruneau, 15, 21; © Steve Krasemann, 18; © J. Cancalosi, 19; © Chris Malazdrewicz, 22; © V. Whelan, 27; © Murray O'Neill, 28; © Don McPhee, 30 (top right); © J.A. Wilkinson, 31 (top left); © Wayne Shiels, 31 (bottom right)
COVER: Boy and cat